Big Crunch: Invisible Apocalyptic Machines

A Glimpse into How the Universe Works

ahmet yazici

Published by ahmet yazici, 2022.

BIG CRUNCH: INVISIBLE APOCALYPTIC MACHINES

First edition. August 27, 2022.

ISBN: 979-8201806606

Written by ahmet yazici.

Also by ahmet yazici

A Glimpse into How the Universe Works
Big Crunch: Invisible Apocalyptic Machines
An Islamic Approach to Time Travel

A Glimpse into the Unseen Realms
Unmaterial Molds
How to Understand the Soul: Spirit or Brain?
How Can Soothsayers Predict the Future?

End Times, Rise of Antichrist (Dajjal), and Golden Age
The Return of Jesus: Conquest of Rome
Armies of the Heavens: Divine Help in Wars

Standalone
Can God Create a Rock He Cannot Lift?: Omnipotence
Paradox

Wouldn't Eternal Life in Paradise Be Boring?: Life in Heaven
Do Humans and Apes Have the Same Ancestors?: Evolution
and Creation in Light of Striking Similarities
Do All Uncovered Women Go to Hell?
Is Coronavirus a Divine Warning?
Is the Quran the Word of God?
Who Created the Mobile Phone?
Why Did Islamic Countries Lag Behind?: Is Islam Not the
Right Religion?

Table of Contents

To Muhammad Samir, Aykut Canturk, Engin Demir,
Ahmed Shakir...

Introduction

The countdown to the apocalypse has begun.

It's like a ticking time bomb with ten seconds to go off. That's why we experience the truth that time speeds up when the apocalypse approaches.

From time to time, different fields of the scientific world make statements such as, "A thousand years later, our earth will be in this situation; 10 million years later, the sun will be like this; this country will be in this situation, etc." What if I told you that the world doesn't have a life span of 200 years?

Just as they do the countdown from 10 on New Year's Eve according to world time (I disapprove), we are about to count down from 10 for the apocalypse according to universe time.

The Prophet (PBUH) said: "The lifespan of my Ummah will not extend past 1500 years."

The caliphate was abolished. The Islamic world was devastated. Europe, which trembled with fear when even hearing the name of the Ottoman Empire, started to realize all kinds of dirty ambitions in Islamic countries. (I mean the cruel face of Europe. All of Europe is not cruel, of course.) Turkey, the grandchild of the Ottoman Empire that ruled three continents, has been struggling for half a century to enter the European Union. Since the caliphate was abolished, the most worthless life in the world has become Muslim life. Fortunately, the caliphate will be established again in this century. There will be a period of peace and abundance throughout the world. (I have touched on these issues in my book "The Return of Jesus". However, to address an important truth about the signs of the apocalypse, I will open a topic on the second coming of Jesus (PBUH) in the following pages.) Unfortunately, the 22nd-century Islamic world will weaken again. This time, the Islamic world will not experience a period of rising. Since the Qur'an and Islam are not in demand among people, Allah will destroy the earth. The world was created to serve God on it. It will be closed when not used for its intended purpose.

The reason I said that the apocalypse will break in the 22nd century is specifically to indicate that there is a short time left before the apocalypse. In this regard, it is necessary to look at the interpretations of Islamic scholars and especially hadith scholars. When we look at the hadiths, it is seen that there are many different narrations about the same subject. The reason for this is that each word was said to a different person at a different time and in a different maqam. Those who will deduce meaning from all these hadiths are Islamic scholars and especially hadith scholars. For example, there is a hadith stating that the world is on the ox and fish. I will open a chapter about this hadith in the following pages. Islamic scholars have given some dates for the apocalypse. The year 2129 is one of them. Indeed, 100 years ago, at the beginning of the 20th century, we faced many calamities, especially the world war. At the beginning of this century, we are experiencing many problems at the global level. The 22nd century might be complete destruction. However, the exact date is in Allah's eternal knowledge. Just as a person feels that his time is approaching, so it is felt as the doomsday approaches. However, at the very beginning of the apocalypse, people will be completely heedless. Consider an earthquake that happens unexpectedly. Imagine a place in the world that has never experienced an earthquake. And while the people of this town weren't even thinking about the earthquake, imagine that the ground shook violently.

It is mentioned that the Quran will be removed from the earth before the apocalypse. All written, digital, and audio, and all formats of that time, will be erased. When the sun rises from the west, people will understand the truth. They will believe in Allah, but it will not be accepted. Maybe people will get used to the sun rising in the west after a while. And when they least expect it, the apocalypse will catch them.

They ask thee about the (final) Hour - when will be its appointed time? Say: "The knowledge thereof is with my Lord (alone): None but He can reveal as to when it will occur. Heavy were its burden through the heavens and the earth. Only, all of a sudden will it come to you." They ask thee as if thou Wert eager in search thereof: Say: "The knowledge thereof is with Allah (alone), but most men know not." (Surah Al-A'raf, Verse 187)

The approaching ˹Hour˺ has drawn near. (Surah An-Najm, Verse 57)

Do they then only wait for the Hour,- that it should come on them of a sudden? But already have come some tokens thereof, and when it (actually) is on them, how can they benefit then by their admonition? (Surah Muhammad, Verse 18)

To Allah belongeth the Mystery of the heavens and the earth. And the Decision of the Hour (of Judgment) is as the twinkling of an eye, or even quicker: for Allah hath power over all things. (Surah An-Nahl, Verse 77)

After this introduction, let's move on to the subject of the apocalypse. In this work, I will talk about how the apocalypse can break out in terms of causes. God created the universe gradually and with wisdom. He could have created it in an instant if He wanted to. It is very easy for the universe to perish. If Allah stopped the reflection of His light and power for a moment, then the universe would not exist. However, He will not destroy the universe in this way. I will prepare a doomsday scenario for you based on hadiths and scientific knowledge. Of course, the horror of the apocalypse is unlike anything. Only God knows how it will break. I aim to prove that the apocalypse is as possible as rain and to convince those who deny the apocalypse.

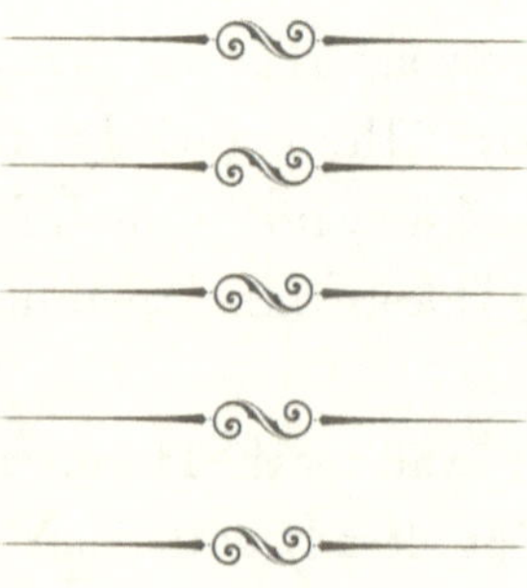

Is it Possible for the Apocalypse to Break out?

Yes. The apocalypse is as natural and possible as rain. The strangest thing is that the apocalypse has not yet broken.

The event we call Doomsday is simply the death of the world. There are countless possibilities for the world to die. But God is protecting us.

Let's imagine. Our earth is full of fire (magma layer). The land we live on is as thin as the shell of an egg. So our world is like a big egg filled with fire.

Let's look at the sky. One comet is all it takes for the world to die.

The earth and other planets are connected to the sun by very delicate balances. They are connected to each other by very sensitive gravitational and repulsive forces. In this way, they neither disperse into space nor enter the body of the sun. What if a cosmic explosion or other cosmic event affects these delicate forces and the perfect balance is disturbed? This perfect balance is not only valid in the solar system. The entire Milky Way galaxy is connected to each other by delicate balances. The enormous gravitational force at the center of our galaxy prevents stars from scattering into space.

It is said that there are millions of black holes even in our Milky Way galaxy. It is even said that there are more black holes than the stars seen in our universe. Since there are 200 billion visible stars even in our Milky Way galaxy, perhaps we are one step away from the apocalypse. Moreover, there are super black holes (I'll talk about black holes in particular) in the universe that have a mass 17 billion times more than the Sun. There are things more terrifying than black holes. Think about quasars, trillions of times brighter than our sun. Quasars are one of the strongest, brightest, and most dangerous objects in the universe. They are such destroyers that they can tear galaxies apart. Beam quasars are even more dangerous. They are incomparable to almost anything else in the universe. These are like beam weapons. These beams travel at millions of kilometers per second. Imagine the power of trillions of stars combined into a beam weapon. The temperature of this beam is trillions of degrees and it pierces the galaxies. There is nothing in the universe that they cannot destroy. If a super quasar approached our galaxy, we wouldn't even be aware we were dead. Our solar system instantly turns into steam.

Allah has created the universe so large (it is estimated to be 96 billion light years) that we have never encountered the danger of a quasar or a black hole until now. (It is so vast that not a single stellar accident has been recorded, even though galaxies have merged through each other.) Terrible cosmic events such as the supernova explosion have not occurred within the distance to affect us. Even if our solar system was at the very end of the sphere of influence of such cosmic events, it would adversely affect life on earth. Fortunately, we are unlikely to encounter a Quasar, too. However, we still have no escape from the apocalypse. The destruction process, which started suddenly, with or without a reason, will surround the world. Meteor, the disturbance of the energy balances of the universe, or the collapse of solar system and galactic systems. The apocalypse begins somehow. Allah knows the truth!

The Almighty Allah has arranged the universe according to a certain plan. All stars and celestial systems move according to this plan. The sun doesn't travel randomly either. All planets included in the system and our old world also participate in the movement of the Sun due to its gravitational power. The Sun is moving at a speed of 20 kilometers per second towards the star VEGA which is near the Sign of Hercules. It has been revealed that this movement of the Sun takes place in a way that makes an angle of 37 degrees with the North Pole Axis. This angle is called the "solar apex". The Quran indicates in Surah Ya-Sin verse 38 that the solar system is collectively heading towards Shams-us'Shumus (sun of suns): "And the sun runs [on course] toward its stopping point. That is the determination of the Exalted in Might, the Knowing."

One of the meanings in this verse is as follows: The sun is flowing towards a time and place determined for it (until the moment it will stop, the Day of Judgment). When the sun reaches the place and time that has been determined for it in pre-eternity, death will catch it and therefore our world.

Examples can be multiplied. Just as the death of man cannot be denied, the death of the earth cannot be denied.

How will the Apocalypse Break out?

There is an extremely delicate order in the universe, from the atom to the stars. It is as if the celestial bodies and systems are connected to each other with invisible strings. The vibration spreading to the universe with the blowing of the trumpet by Israfil (peace be upon him) disrupts the delicate order. The strings of attraction and repulsion are broken. Stars and planets are scattered like rosary beads. The balance in the universe is disrupted; galactic systems begin to collapse. The universe apartment begins to crack, waver, and collapse.

To Allah ˹alone˺ belongs ˹the knowledge of˺ the unseen in the heavens and the earth. Bringing about the Hour would only take the blink of an eye, or even less. Surely Allah is Most Capable of everything. (Surah an-Nahl, Verse 77) The verse indicates: the final end will occur at a time that humanity has not yet anticipated, and that everything will occur in an instant. The earth will be thrown out, mountains and seas will be thrown into space, and the earth will turn into a dust heap.

O humanity! Fear your Lord, for the ˹violent˺ quaking at the Hour is surely a dreadful thing. (Surah Al-Hajj, Verse 1)

The world's largest recorded earthquake is the Chile Earthquake. Its magnitude is 9.5. What if the earthquake that brings about the apocalypse will be 13 magnitude? Perhaps even larger. Imagine the intensity of such an earthquake. The apocalyptic scenes described in the Quran will come to life before your eyes. According to geologists, even a 10-magnitude earthquake is almost impossible to occur. An earthquake of 10 magnitude may be impossible until the moment of doomsday. However, the Day of Judgment, the day of the death of the universe, is a terrifying day when the impossible will become possible. The earth will ripple like the sea. Mountains will crumble from their foundations. The mountains will be broken into pieces and scattered like flour. The earth will be flat. The ground will crack and split into pieces; perhaps countless islands will emerge. Flames will gush from the cracked ground. The earth will fall into magma. Magma will swallow the whole earth. There is not a single piece of land left to step on. The waters in the oceans are mixed with magma. Earth now looks like an angry, glowing fireball. The Earth returns to its state before it was filled with living creatures and people. Now the world is a huge sea of fire and a ball of fire. Flames covered the sky. Fire is pouring from the sky. The seas and oceans are flowing over people as if they were emptying from the skies. The seas are boiling. The ground is collapsing. Lava erupts from the collapsing ground on people. It is such a terrifying day that (let's assume) a world war broke out and nuclear bombs exploded en masse, perhaps it would not be noticed. Neither the earth nor the sky pities man. Wouldn't it be unfair to show compassion and mercy to those who oppress, who create mischief in the world for the sake of their own interests, who shed blood, who invent new diseases for the sake of their own interests, who make humanity sick by changing the genetics of crops, and who commit many other terrible acts? There is no place to run.

By no means! No place of safety! (Surah Al-Qiyamah, Verse 11)

If there is a magnitude 9.5 earthquake, why not a magnitude 10? Mathematically, it is very close. But according to geologists, it is not. Now let's quote from Live Science to make the earthquake magnitude issue more concrete in our minds.

"How big is the largest possible earthquake?

The amount of energy released in an earthquake is controlled by how much of the crust breaks. The good news is, we're not likely to see a magnitude 10.

On May 22, 1960, a devastating earthquake hit southern Chile... But could quakes get bigger?

The answer, geoscientists say, is yes. However, the chances of a much larger quake are low. While a quake larger in magnitude than 9.5 could occur, it would require an enormous chunk of crust to break all at once — the movement of a fault both enormously deep and extraordinarily long. There aren't many places on Earth where that could happen, said Wendy Bohon, an earthquake geologist and science communicator. A 9.5 magnitude quake is probably right around the upper limit for what the planet can generate, Bohon told Live Science, and a magnitude 10 is extremely unlikely.

The earthquake magnitude scale can inadvertently obscure the difference between very large earthquakes. The scale isn't linear, but logarithmic: For every unit it goes up, the ground motion increases 10 times and the energy released goes up 32 times. Bohon likes to use the metaphor of breaking a bundle of spaghetti. If breaking one strand of spaghetti is the equivalent of a magnitude 5 earthquake, you'd have to break 32 strands to release the energy of a magnitude 6 quake. On this spaghetti scale, a magnitude 7 is like 1,024 strands breaking, a magnitude 8 is like 32,768 strands, and a magnitude 9 is like 1,048,576 strands." (By Stephanie Pappas, published January 30, 2023)

Today is the time to be abandoned by the beloved of humankind, who spends all the love in his heart on the temporary world. The result of illegitimate love is torment without mercy.

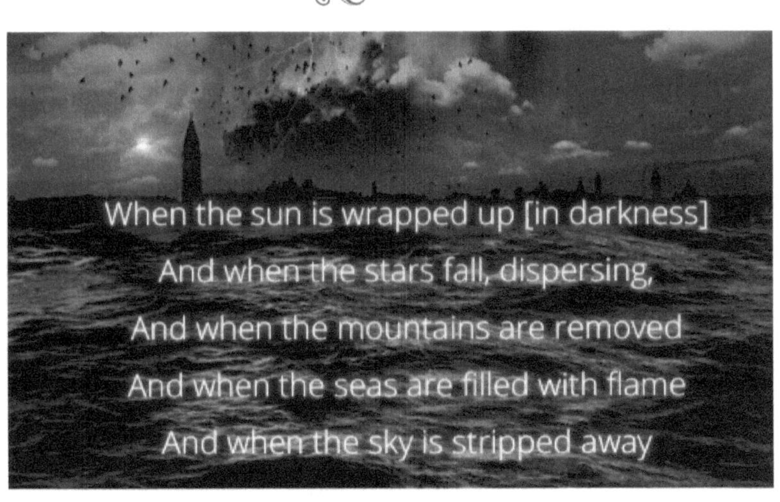

QUESTION: SO HOW WILL people who die immediately experience the horrors of the apocalypse?

Answer: Every living thing witnesses the horrors of the apocalypse until they die. They continue to see with their spirit eyes even after death. Souls in the intermediate realm also watch the destruction.

Everyone will see the apocalypse. But everyone will be affected to their degree. Those who will experience the horror of the apocalypse with their eyes are those who were alive when the apocalypse broke out. At the time of the Doomsday, the spirits of the people of faith will be taken earlier as a mercy in order not to see the horrors of the Doomsday, and the Doomsday will come upon the unbelievers. As for those who have died before the Day of Judgment, that is, those who are in the grave: The people of punishment will be affected painfully, and the people of happiness will be amazed.

The real addressees of the apocalypse are the non-believers who are alive that day. Even if those who are caught up in the apocalypse die in a short time, they may perceive this period as a very long time due to the terror they are in. Furthermore, after they die, they will continue to watch the horrific scenes of the apocalypse from a different perspective and will continue to be affected and feel to the first degree. Above all, Allah is able to create time within time. Allah will deal with these unbelievers, who bring the apocalypse upon them with their rebellion, cruelty, and spoiledness, as He wishes.

"THE DAY THAT WE ROLL up the heavens like a scroll rolled up for books (completed)," (Surah Al-Anbya Verse 104)

The Trumpet will (just) be sounded, when all that are in the heavens and on earth will swoon, except such as it will please Allah (to exempt). Then will a second one be sounded, when, behold, they will be standing and looking on! (Surah Az-Zumar, Verse 68) The verb "sa'iqa" in the verse is mostly interpreted as "to die from fear" in tafsir books. It is stated that those who are exempted from the influence of Trumpet are the great angels named Gabriel, Michael, and Azrael. In some narrations, other angels have been added to these, such as the angel named Rıdvan and those who carry the Throne, and those who serve as guards in heaven and hell.

Black Holes Invisible Apocalyptic Machines

By consuming celestial objects, black holes grow larger and more powerful. Begins to swallow with more appetite as it grows stronger. How far will this growth and absorption go is the question. Could the cosmos eventually turn into a black hole?

Death is one of the laws that Allah has set on earth, and it also carries out its judgment in the heavens. New stars are created again from nebulae. Like living things on earth, stars grow and die after a period of development.

Black holes are formed when giant stars die. The center of stars larger than the sun, whose death is approaching, shrinks to the size of a city. Hydrogen ends in the center and after a point, the gravitational force alone becomes dominant in the star. The star center disappears in the universe. At that point, space is now punctured. The star is now a black hole. During this transformation, a supernova explosion occurs, which can throw the outer parts of the star a thousand light-years away.

The centers of the stars are the centers of the creation of the elements. All the elements in our body were once created in the millions of degrees of heat of the stars (Allah created).

This means that our world is not a detachment from the Sun. Because our Earth contains elements of stars that have passed the red giant period. With the supernova explosion, the elements necessary for life were brought down to our world.

Other heavy elements, including the element iron in our world, came from giant stars in outer space. Actually, we were once a part of a star in terms of our material body. That this star must be much larger than our Sun. Astronomical facts explains that iron is only produced at temperatures up to a few hundred million degrees. In other words, it was produced in the ovens of stars much larger than the Sun, to plant the seeds of life on our planet. Our sun, on the other hand, has a reactor temperature of 15 million degrees, and in this case, it is not capable of producing large elements. We are informed in the Qur'an that iron was sent down. "And We sent down iron, wherein there is awesome power and many benefits for people." (Surah al-Hadid, Verse 25)

Could the Gates of Heaven mentioned in the Quran be Black Holes?

The Qur'an draws our attention to the invisible gates of the sky. Is it possible to understand "the gates" as portals to other space-time, different dimensions, and universes because they are places of passage?

He Who created the seven heavens one above another: No want of proportion wilt thou see in the Creation of ((Allah)) Most Gracious. So turn thy vision again: seest thou any flaw? (Surah Al-Mulk, Verse 3)

Space is likened to a stretched web. The above verse indicates that the web of space-time is extremely solid. Heavy objects are placed on the web, and it bends. And the space-time web (space) is bent and twisted in the same way by the massive celestial bodies "sitting" on it. The black hole, which means an infinite weight, bends the space-time web in that region. It is not satisfied with this, it tears and pierces the web of space-time. The laws of physics are no longer valid there; the door to the metaphysical realm has been opened.

Black holes are depicted as a funnel. The widest part of this region is the event horizon. There is also a region where the gravitational effect increases incredibly and becomes almost infinite. This is the tip of the 'funnel' and is called the singularity. Beyond the singularity is a region where laws very different from the physical realm are valid. Black holes may be taking space-time with them by outflowing with their own existence and self-volume. It may be acting as a gateway to different realms where the physical laws in this realm are not valid.

In the singularity of black holes, time slows down incredibly, even stops and freezes. Stopping time means losing the validity of the laws of physics and entering a brand new universe. This new universe will be nothing like our own. Time, matter, and dimensions will be of different quality.

Could these new Universes, which cannot be explained by the narrow patterns of physics, be the realms of the hereafter? Could these be the permanence realms that are very different from the material realms? Badiuzzaman says that some stars are looking into the realms of permanence.

Physicists previously did not consider the existence of universes other than ourselves possible. Studies on cosmic rays have shown that there are rays faster than light. In addition, mathematical equations showed the existence of abstract universes. Calculations made by ignoring abstract spaces were inaccurate. The number of physicists who saw possible the existence of universes composed of abstract elements thousands and millions faster than the speed of light gradually increased.

Developing science has raised new questions about matter and space. In the past, the matter was seen as a god. The life of the deified substance ended very quickly. It turned out that matter and atom were nothing. I have covered this subject in my book "Quantum to Ether". Matter and physical realms, which were thought to be immutable and inviolable, began to be ignored. Black holes have changed not only matter but also the concept of time.

Questions that used to be asked in religious conversations and ridiculed by materialist circles are now being discussed in the most modern astronomy centers.

Black holes, which are tunnels and paths that can go out of space, give us clues in interpreting some hadiths about the apocalypse. I will give the hadiths, which are our subject, in terms of their meaning. With these clues, we can make some evaluations of the concepts of "Majerra and Shams-us'Shumus ".

The following words of our Prophet (PBUH) are mentioned in the records of San'ani, who is accepted as the first hadith author: "The days were presented to me. I saw Friday; I liked its beauty and its light. I saw something in the form of a black dot there. 'What is this?' I asked. It was said, 'Doomsday will break within it." In another version of the hadith, it is stated as follows: "It was shown to me in a mirror on Friday."

What is meant by the "black dot" in the hadith, in which it is stated that the apocalypse will break out? And the heaven is opened and will become gateways (Surah an-Naba, Verse 19).

When the sky is rent asunder, And hearkens to (the Command of) its Lord, and it must needs (do so) (Surah Al-Inshiqaq, Verse 1-2)

Hazrat Ali (may Allah be pleased) said that the sky would crack and split from "Majerra". Thanks to the developments in space science, we can grasp these reports more easily. Black holes can crack and pierce the networked and solidly established space. With our current knowledge, we can interpret the "split in the sky" indicated by the verses as the opening of doors to different dimensions by changing the physical world, namely space-time.

He Who created the seven heavens one above another: No want of proportion wilt thou see in the Creation of (Allah) Most Gracious. So turn thy vision again: seest thou any flaw? (Surah Al-Mulk, Verse 3) In this verse, Allah clearly states that heaven, that is, the physical universe called space-time, is in a solid structure and is free of cracks. However, in the verses about the apocalypse, it is constantly emphasized that cracking will occur in the sky. One day the earth will be changed to a different earth, and so will be the heavens, and (men) will be marshalled forth, before Allah, the One, the Irresistible (Surah Ibrahim, Verse 48). In this verse, it is stated that when Doomsday breaks, the door to the hereafter will be opened with these cracks.

THE BLACK HOLE THAT can cause galaxy-wide destruction is located at the center of the galaxy. Astronomers believe that every Galaxy has a supermassive black hole at its center. There is an extraordinary activity in the center of the Milky Way. Celestial objects 200 light years from the center of the galaxy have a speed of 1000 km. per second. Such a high velocity so far from the center can only be caused by the central mass being 2 million times greater than the sun. It is thought that there is a supermassive black hole at the center of our galaxy, too. This black hole, Sagittarius A, the sun of our galaxy, is 27 thousand light-years away from the Earth. It is estimated to have a mass equal to four million Suns. We can compare the weight of black holes with neutron stars weighing as much as 40 billion tons in a teaspoon. Black holes are hundreds of thousands of times heavier than neutron stars. And it has gravitational power in proportion to its weight. The black hole in the center of the Milky Way continues to swallow and grows and becomes stronger as it swallows, and its sphere of influence is increasing. Our Solar System is approaching the area of influence of this giant monster at a speed of 50 km every second.

Let's imagine a huge dam. Let's make small breaches in various parts of the dam wall. The waters of the dam will make pressure and widen these gaps over time. After a certain point, the wall of the dam will collapse completely. Likewise, we can think of black holes as breaches that carry this realm to other realms. (currently carrying this universe to other realms slowly, just like a breach in a dam) One day, these breaches may open completely and swallow the whole universe, or they may empty the entire universe into other realms.

One day, all black holes may become one giant black hole. That day is the hardest in the universe, the Day of Judgment.

And to Allah belongs the dominion of the heavens and the earth, and to Allah is the destination.

THE DAY OF THE RESURRECTION comes. Almighty Allah will change the heavens and the earth, create a new world, and everything will be level. With the call of Allah, all beings will be restored to their original state. By Allah's command, it will rain from the heavens for forty days. Then Allah will order the bodies to be resurrected. The corpses will come out of the ground like the greening of plants. Then God will call all souls. Allah fills all souls in Trumpet and commands Israfil. Israfil obeys the order and blows the Trumpet. Spirits coming out of Trumpet fill the space between heaven and earth. Then God commands each soul to enter its own corpse. After the souls enter the corpses, the ground splits and everyone leaves their graves and starts walking towards the gathering place.

The force that draws the world to itself is not only the black hole in the center of the galaxy. I mentioned in the previous pages that the sun also has a unique movement. The Sun is in motion at a speed of 20 kilometers per second towards the star VEGA, which was near the Sign of Hercules.

The Solar System shows some deviation in its movement towards the center of the galaxy. Could the force causing this deflection be another black hole? And moreover, can it be said that there is another black hole to prevent this deviation? So maybe there are many black holes trying to swallow our solar system.

Considering that there are one million black holes in the arms of the Milky Way alone, we can say that a black hole can appear at any time and everywhere.

Our Sun is alone, unlike other suns. Our Sun must have a twin. So where is the peer of the sun? Astronomers think that the Sun's peer turned into a black hole early on.

The sun is heading towards Shams-us'Shumus with its planets. Perhaps Shams-us'Shumus was the peer of the Sun. Assuming it was a much larger star than the sun, it died early and turned into a black hole. And it attracts his peer, the Sun. Large stars run out of fuel quickly and die earlier than smaller stars; and they turn into a black hole.

A star that becomes a black hole pulls its peer towards itself and eventually swallows it whole. There are many examples of this phenomenon in space.

Badiuzzaman is of the opinion that the worlds subject to Shams-us'Shumus are from the eternal realm. Also, he is of the opinion that one day in the current time flow in Shams-us'Shumus is equal to fifty thousand years according to our measurements... Time has expanded extraordinarily in the realms subject to Shams-us'Shumus. This measure of time is mentioned in the Quran for the speed of angels. Based on all the topics we have covered, if we assume that Shams-us'Shumus is from the realms of afterlife and eternity, or that it looks at the eternal realms, we can deduce the possibility that Shams-us'Shumus is a black hole and that it is the gateway to the parallel realms, that is, to the realms of eternal. In other words, perhaps because it turned into a black hole, it transitioned to the eternal realms with its subordinate planets. Astrophysicists, too, think that black holes may be a gateway to get out of this universe prison.

The stars cannot escape death too. Since no particle in this universe will go to extinction; the corpses of stars that died in the space sea will also be swept away by black holes and pushed into the eternal realms. When the apocalypse breaks and the universe is recreated, these particles will take on new duties in the hereafter. According to Badiuzzaman, the heat of the stars comes from hell and their light comes from heaven. In other words, even now, the realms of the hereafter have duties they undertake in this universe. On the Day of Judgment, the Sun will be included in Hell and will burn those who worship it.

ONCE OUR SOLAR SYSTEM enters the black hole's gravitational field, we can no longer talk about gravity as we know it. The mountains begin to move and crumble, and the oceans begin to swell. Gases in the atmosphere completely fly into space, and the layers of the atmosphere become dysfunctional. The air on earth becomes unsuitable for living things.

THIS VAST UNIVERSE will undoubtedly collapse one day, just as the stars crackle and collapse into themselves.

THREATS TO OUR WORLD and our solar system are not limited to these. There is such a black hole that it threatens our entire galaxy. The Milky Way galaxy, which is estimated to contain at least 200 billion stars, is going somewhere at an indescribable speed. The Milky Way is rapidly drifting at 700 kilometers per second into a region beyond the Hydra-Centaurus galaxy 300 million light-years away. There is a black hole in this region with an extraordinary gravitational pull, large enough to contain tens of thousands of galaxies. This black hole is called the "Great Attractor" because of its extraordinary gravitational pull. Astronomers say that 900 galaxies fell under the influence of this Great Attractor and were drifting towards it at terrifying speeds. But what if there are millions of black holes like the Great Attractor in the universe?

According to some scientists, our Galaxy is not only being pulled, but also pushed. By "dark matter". I have already mentioned that the objects in the space are connected by extremely sensitive ropes of attraction and continue to stay in their orbits by pulling and pushing forces. It is not surprising that dark matter, or any other unproven matter, repels objects in the space. As I mentioned in my book "Quantum to Ether", space is not empty.

———— ❧ ————

IT SEEMS THAT AS LONG as space exploration continues, space will continue to amaze us with all its grandeur and beauty.

———— ❧ ————

RETURNING TO THE SUBJECT of Mejerra that we talked about in the previous pages, according to some commentators, mejerra is the Milky Way. The expressions related to Mejerra (It is written in Turkish as "mecerra". It may be spelled "majarra" in English.") are as follows:

"Mejerra" is the sky gate, from which the sky will be split.

"The "mejerra" in the sky is the sweat (saliva) of the snake under the throne." The hadith differs a little bit in another version. This hadith mentions that the Prophet (PBUH) said to Muaz (may Allah be pleased) when he sent him to Yemen to serve as governor-general: "I am sending you to a stubborn people. When questioned about the mejerra in the sky, he advised to respond, "It is the serpent's saliva under the Throne." Some hadith experts viewed the claim that these two words belonged to the Prophet (PBUH) as weak, and some even viewed it as a fabrication. Unlike other hadiths about mejerra, neither of these two hadiths mentions the gates of the heavens. The expecting questions from the Yemenis show that the Milky Way nebula or the galaxy was a topic of interest at that time. We are unable to understand what is meant by the snake and its sweat and saliva, even if we accept the hadiths to be authentic. As is common knowledge, however, some star groups have traditionally been called by animal names. Mejerra might be compared to a snake's head. Or it might be compared to its entirely ingesting a massive prey with its small head. This response, which is attributed to the Prophet, makes it apparent that anything outside the Milky Way is being intended.

Although it is not known whether this hadith is authentic, it expresses a truth.

Most often through similes and metaphors, Our Prophet (PBUH) conveyed the complex and profound realities that were challenging to comprehend at the time. The word "snake" is one of the most suitable comparisons to be made for black holes. Black holes are referred to as "wormholes" in the scientific community because of their ability to connect two spaces in the shape of a tunnel hose. According to its size, the snake can swallow huge objects, which it then transfers down a long, slender tunnel. The term implies that black holes are passageways leading from the visible realm to the Throne.

If the invisible sky doors are black holes, the afterlife realms may not be as far away as we think. Of course, what I mean by the realms of the afterlife are not heaven and hell. First and foremost, I mean the other layers of the sky, that if black holes are a gateway connected to the Throne, we wouldn't be wrong if we said that even though heaven is very far from us, it is close.

Black holes can also be used as shortcuts to travel between all celestial layers. Or universe highways, or airlines... It can transport us to galaxies billions of light-years away in record time. In this sense, it is an intergalactic highway.

Of course, based on our current knowledge, black holes do not appear to be a safe haven for humans. It is possible that there are beings who use these terrible tunnels, which we are unable to use.

The jinn were able to ascend to such heights in the heavens that they could hear the angels. I covered this topic in my book "Hidden Treasures: A Glimpse To The Unseen Realms". How did they get here if we assume their journey took them up to the limits of the second Heaven? Total travel time for the Jinn to approach the second Heaven's boundaries; billions of years. This is impossible without black holes.

As the geometric gravity balance deteriorates, the space-time flatness of the heavens can be rolled up and crumpled like a piece of paper, as expressed in the Qur'an, and the stars fall from their places. Because the celestial bodies are delicately linked with the attraction ropes. The enormous gravitational force of black holes is powerful enough to upset these equilibriums.

With billions of stars and planets in it, each galaxy must include unimaginable strong spots that will eventually destroy it and then recreate it in a different creation. Understanding enormous powers and the skills they possess is not simple. They are not stray, though. The only divine power that gave them strength and created them holds the reins over them. It will be clear who explains the Quranic words more accurately after science advances.

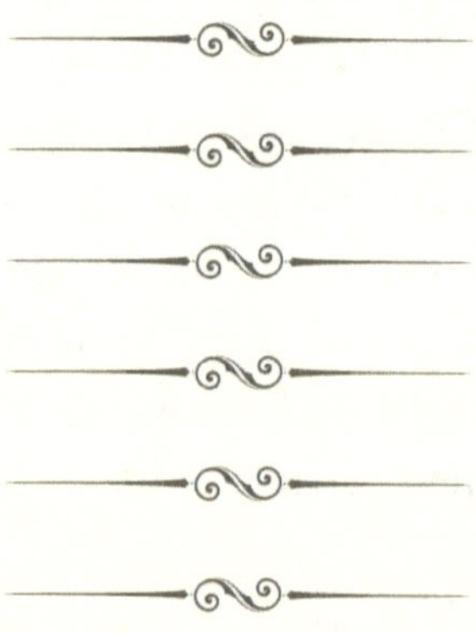

Mystery at the Center of our Galaxy

There could be something at the center of our galaxy that is more enigmatic than a black hole. It's possible that a dark matter cluster rather than a supermassive black hole is at the center of our galaxy.

The center of the Milky Way galaxy is thought to contain a supermassive black hole, but a recent study raises the possibility that there may be something even more mysterious there.

Because of how stars revolve around it, the huge object Sagittarius A at the galactic center has always been referred to be a "black hole."

The G2 gas cloud's nearness to the black hole, however, called into doubt this presumption. Scientists had anticipated that the powerful gravitational pull of Sagittarius A would destroy the cloud, but this did not occur, and G2 lived on without incident.

The supermassive black hole remains the most widely accepted theory for our galaxy's core, but the truth may be more complicated than we thought. Some scientists believe that supermassive black holes, in particular, may consist of dark matter.

Scientific research is a bottomless pit. Each new research and invention renders the previous ones obsolete.

Some researchers now believe that Sagittarius A is a collection of dark matter rather than a black hole. We will continue to discover new mysteries as long as space exploration continues!

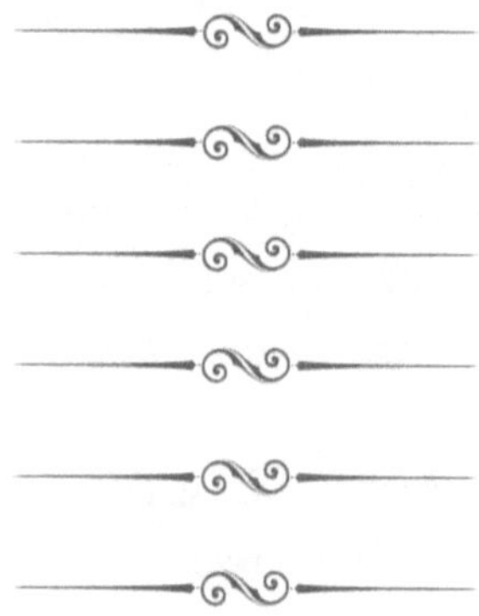

White Holes and Birth of the Universe

What comes after a black hole's singularity? White Holes are scientists' first guess. Their predictions are as follows: A black hole's singularity has merged with another universe's singularity to form a narrow tunnel shaped like an hourglass. The white hole of another universe is its singularity. White holes, unlike black holes, do not consume everything around them. Rather, they blast out anything that comes their way. In contrast to black holes, these extremely bright regions have pushing and lifting rather than pulling.

When time is reversed, we see that an initial space-time singularity representing the "big bang" is unavoidable. This time, the singularity represents the creation of all matter and space-time rather than its destruction. This is a white hole singularity. There is complete time symmetry between these two singularities. The first type of singularity is a white hole, from which space-time and matter are created. The final type of singularity is a black hole, in which space, time, and matter vanish.

It is as possible for white holes not to exist as it is for them to exist. Black holes are the graves of stars. Black holes will most likely trigger the apocalypse. Black holes can also be worlds of non-existence (nothingness). In that case, white holes may not exist at all. That objects drawn into black holes go to the realms of non-existence does not mean they will be destroyed forever. Because Allah, who records everything, will recreate that object. Let's say a person falls into a black hole. The soul never dies. The body disappears. Since the relationship between the soul and the body is not completely severed, a person who falls into a black hole can experience his body going to the realm of non-existence to some extent through his immortal soul. This nothingness may be for a very short time, even momentarily. In other words, under normal conditions, when a person dies, the body and soul continue to be in contact. However, as an exception, the body and soul connection may suddenly be cut off because the body of someone who dies in a black hole will be destroyed. In this case, the soul may experience the destruction of the body with astonishment. But the soul will never die. Of course, Allah will resurrect that body on the day of judgment. What I mean is, supposing there are no white holes, black holes may be worlds of non-existence. There may be worlds working on behalf of the worlds of non-existence. Allah created the universe from nothing. If scientists can send unmanned vehicles into black holes in the future, they may find clues about how the universe came into being from nothing. Perhaps we will reveal many secrets about the universe soon.

Big Crunch

Allah will fold and roll up the vast skies like rolling up scrolls of paper.

THE UNIVERSE IS ALWAYS expanding since the day Almighty Allah created it out of nothing. He will roll it back to its previous with His infinite power on the Day of the Resurrection. Then He will create a new realm appropriate for the life to come.

With His infinite power, Allah will gather back the countless stars and galaxies by wrapping them in sheets again, which He brought out of the realm of non-existence into the field of existence by laying the matter of Ether like a sheet.

The Qur'an explains that creation will return to the state in which it was first started. Studies on the moon and meteorites show that the earth and sky were once in one piece before disintegrating and becoming what they are today.

THE EXISTING ORDER will be destroyed when the apocalypse occurs. The celestial bodies are brought together, stacked and folded like pages of a book, and restored to their initial form.

Then a new order is constructed that provides the circumstances and setting necessary for an immortal life in the afterlife. The systems that are in place now are designed to keep people alive for a while. The afterlife has an endless existence. In that regard, the new order that will be founded needs to have a plan and program that will address this.

Then He turned towards the heaven when it was ⸢still like⸣ smoke, saying to it and to the earth, 'Submit, willingly or unwillingly.' They both responded, 'We submit willingly.' (Surah Fussilat, Verse 11)

According to the Qur'an, the earth and heavens were once one contiguous smoky mass, which was later split to form the heavens and earth.

The mass in question was divided into major parts to form the heavens. These large pieces were then divided into smaller pieces that would eventually form stars, planets, and other objects.

PIECES THAT SPLIT OFF from a mass moved away from each other. According to what we understand from the Qur'an, after the expansion is finished, the return will start. The heavens or galaxies will return to the contiguous mass, or single point, state from which they initially separated. A massive mass of dust will erupt as a result of the collision of all stars, planets, and galaxies bursting out of their orbits. This will most likely be in a nebula structure, like the initial beginning.

The heavens and earth, which opened like an umbrella with the big bang, will close with the big crunch and be brought back together at the first point of opening. They'll pile up to this point in a cloud of shattered dust and smoke. According to the Qur'an, which describes every sky or galaxy as a page of a book, these opened pages will eventually be folded by being rolled up to the point where they first opened, or to a specific line.

The collapse of an entire sky and galaxies or entire sky levels at one point will perhaps create a much more terrifying sight than the first explosion.

A universe core will consist as a result of (universe) being folded, and closed to a point. A core will exist for the universe's re-creation, just as the tree and man (tail bone) both have one. This core will wait till it reopens and explodes one day.

With the rollup, the earth, moon and other planets will be included in the sun. The solar system will merge with our galaxy, and this process will continue until the entire universe collapses into a single nucleus. Even if the Earth merges with the other planets and stars in the sky, the essence of all humans and other living things will be preserved in its own substance. Among the rolled-up pages, Earth will be a very special page.

⌜How horrible will it be⌝ when the heavens will split apart, becoming rose-red like ⌜burnt⌝ oil! (Surah Ar-Rahman, Verse 37)

Commentators on the 37th verse of Surah Rahman have always focused on the color of the skies rather than shape and form. Many commentators, beginning with Ibn Abbas, deduced from the verse in question that the skies would turn the color of a red horse at that time.

THE HEAVENS WILL CONSTITUTE a crimson mass or point, as well as a rose-shaped mass or point. All the power of the heavens is concentrated in this mass. The heavens may have been transformed into a completely invisible power (energy) separate from the matter at this point. However, even if a power does not manifest itself, it still exists, and it is incorrect to refer to it as absent. This incredible power point and the red bud of the universe will await Almighty Allah's command before opening up and spreading out to form new heavens and realms.

The universe was created from an infinitely dense and infinitely thin point of light, with a burst of light (white hole).

The beginning of the universe was the big bang, and the end will be the big crunch.

Under the influence of gravity, this vast expanding universe will begin to spin back and contract. The galaxies will begin to approach each other like rolling a piece of paper in the palm of one's hand. While each galaxy is swallowed by giant black holes at its center, the rotation speed of galaxies will gradually increase. As a result, while billions of galaxies become super giant black holes, black holes will collide with "approaching infinity speed" and become hyper-giant black holes.

This is the point of light (white hole) where matter ceases to be matter, as it becomes infinitely thinner. The light point is infinitely dense, infinitely thin, zero-dimensional, zero-volume, and ready to explode. This is the nucleus of the final big bang (I used the big bang expression because it is a scientific term.), with which the universe will be created once more.

ANOTHER BIG CRUNCH scenario could be that the latent dark energy that encompasses most of the universe is withdrawn from the universe and the universe collapses. It collapses like a large building with its columns cut or the dome of a large mosque with its balance stone removed. Likewise, if Allah pulls back the force He has sent to the electrons, all the wheels of the universe clock will break apart; all particles of matter will eject from their places, and the universe's cries of terror will echo in space. During the apocalypse, these collapse scenarios will occur sequentially or simultaneously, suddenly or over a period of time. The discretion belongs to Allah.

IF ALLAH WERE TO ABRUPTLY cut off the electricity simultaneously flowing to the stars and galaxies, the stars would dim like lamps, cease their movements, and start to fall one by one.

WHEN ALLAH ROLLS UP the universe, will he destroy the objects completely?

Islamic scholars have different opinions on this issue.

According to some scholars: "Allah will scatter the atoms of bodies, but will not destroy them. Then Allah will recombine them."

According to another group: "Allah will completely destroy objects and then recreate them as the same substance."

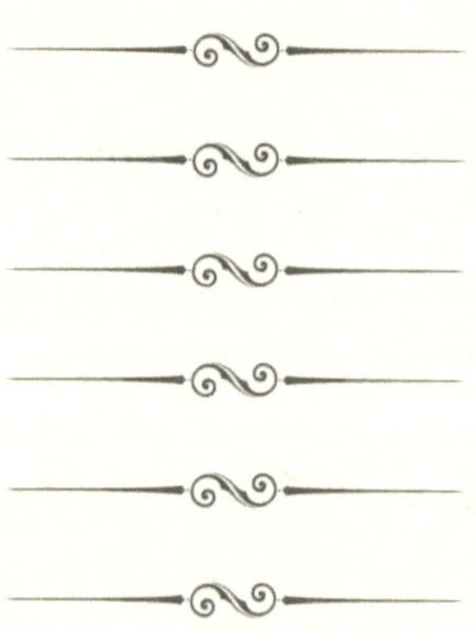

Why didn't Jesus (PBUH) Come?

Let's assume.

The sun rose from the west.

Wouldn't Jesus (PBUH) come before the apocalypse?

The answer is very simple. Jesus (PBUH) descended from heaven. He lived on Earth for the second time. And he died. But people didn't know.

Why didn't they know?

Because people were waiting for Jesus (PBUH) to be on the news.

Jesus (PBUH) will not make statements in the important political institutions of the world.

Jesus (PBUH) will not come as a prophet but as a saint. That's why he won't announce his arrival.

Even those closest to him will not be completely sure that he is Jesus (PBUH).

I'm quoting from my book "The Return of Jesus: Conquest of Rome" about why individuals such as the Antichrist, Mahdi, and Jesus (PBUH) (major signs of the apocalypse) could not be seen clearly:

There are countless mysteries and wisdom to hide some tidings of Ghayb (nonvisible, unknown) about the future till a certain time. For example, since a person's time of death is concealed, he keeps both death and ongoing life in his mind, and he works for both this world and the Hereafter. He knows also that the Day of Judgment may come at any age, so he works for eternal life and also tries to build the world as if he will never die. Likewise; if a man were informed of disasters or of his death in advance, he would suffer many times more than the actual disaster and death. But since he does not know the day of his death, he can live joyfully.

Some individuals like Dajjal and Mahdi are secret in order for people to choose their place in the fight between truth and falsehood. This world has been a fighting arena between the truth and the falsehood since Adam (PBUH). Namroods and Pharaohs in history were Dajjal. Each century has a specific Dajjal.

Religion is a test. The God Almighty keeps some things secret depending on some wisdom. God eventually will separate the people who turn their spirit to white from people who turn their spirit to black. In this way, Abu Bakr may rise to the highest of the high, and Abu Jahl may descend to the lowest of the low. If the answers to the questions become clear, we can not make this distinction. Hence, since religion is a test, every issue related to religion is evaluated within the framework of the examination. For example, people have the obligation to believe in the Prophet (PBUH). But even though he was a prophet, and he had miracles, the door was opened to the mind, and free will was not taken away. So people were not forced to believe. Prophet Muhammad (PBUH) split the moon in two. Yet some did not accept Islam. Allah did not force anyone to believe, and He did not take the free will away. There is no value in compulsory belief. The events also related to the end of the time occur in a similar way. It's a little more confidential. People can only be aware of the signs of Doomsday if they look carefully at the course of the events. They can be recognized through the light of belief. Divine wisdom necessitates that each century waits for a Mahdi and a Dajjal, and that the people of each century think as if the doom will break out at any time. Those who have weak beliefs and do not plunge into a quest will not see Mahdi and Jesus; even if they see them and are side by side with them, they will not be able to recognize them. However, only the people of wisdom will be able to recognize them through the light of the belief. All the news about the end of the time is obscure and veiled, except one. That is the rising of the sun from the west. This will happen exactly; there is no explanation for this. People will be compelled to believe. After this, it will be not accepted any repentance and belief. The trial and test will be ended. Man does not believe what he sees, he witnesses what he sees. Good quality and valid faith are to believe in the unseen.

Our Lord says concerning faith that: Who believe in the unseen, establish prayer, and spend out of what We have provided for them (Al-Baqarah 2:3)

So how will people know that he is in the world?

There are signs of his being in the world. I explained it in more detail in my book "The Return of Jesus: Conquest of Rome".

As a result, people may be caught in the apocalypse itself while waiting for the great signs of the apocalypse.

Will Everything Perish When Doomsday Strikes?

"Everything (that exists) will perish except His (Allah's) own Face." (Surah Al-Qasas,verse 88)

There is no clear decree on the subject, but some scholars believe that everything will perish when Doomsday arrives.

Some scholars, however, interpreted the word "halikun" in the verse as "perishable." That is, everything was created in a perishable form, but Allah Almighty will destroy something if He wishes. Or He allows it to exist.

"One day the earth will be changed to a different earth, and so will be the heavens, and (men) will be marshalled forth, before Allah, the One, the Irresistible." (Surah Ibrahim, Verse 48)

Based on the knowledge that the earth and heavens would change, the scholars concluded that they would all perish during Doomsday. There is no clear decree among scholars, though, whether this "transformation" will result in the form of total elimination or take on a new form.

The verses and hadiths do not go into detail about how Doomsday will occur and whether or not everyone will perish. However, according to the general opinion accepted by Islamic scholars, the Day of judgment is in question for all beings, not just the solar system.

According to some scholars, the meaning of perish expressed in the verse will not be in the realm of permanence, which includes heaven and hell. In other words, they claim that destruction will only occur in the material realm.

Some scholars say that the act of perish will also occur in the realm of permanence, which includes heaven and hell, in addition to the material realm. But they say that it will happen so quickly that no one will notice its disappearance.

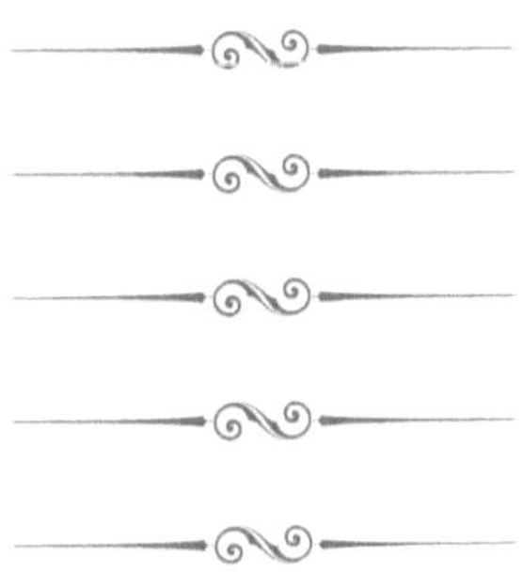

The World is on the Ox and Fish

Is there a hadith stating that the world is on the ox and fish?

If there is, how should we understand it?

Yes, this saying is a hadith. However, the narrations that "the world is on the ox and when the ox shakes its horn, an earthquake occurs" are not hadiths. They are fabricated words.

A statement has three meanings: reality, metaphor, and allusion. It becomes a reality if it is used in the same sense in which it is uttered. It is a metaphor if it is used in a sense other than its own and if there is an impediment to using it in its own sense. And allusion occurs when something is expressed not with its own meaning but with the opposite of that meaning.

For instance, if the word "wooden" is used to describe a material used to manufacture furniture, this is a reality. When used as a metaphor, it means someone who is foolish and thick-headed.

For the subject of what the hadith's intended meaning is: the Earth rests upon an ox and a fish.

With this statement, Prophet Muhammad (PBUH) wished to convey three meanings:

The first is that each creation that God Almighty creates has an angel appointed to it. They are referred to as Appointed Angels. The world too has two appointed angels, Savr (ox) and Hut (fish).

The second is that agriculture and hunting were the two most significant sources of income in the Prophet Muhammad's (PBUH) and his companions' era, which was fourteen centuries ago. This is still partially true. Ox is the emblem of agriculture, and fish is the emblem of hunting. With this hadith, Prophet Muhammad (PBUH) emphasized this truth and identified the two most crucial sources of human sustenance.

Our Prophet (pbuh) has very eloquently expressed the two most important resources in people's livelihood, that is, in the continuation of worldly life. It is fish that represents the sea, and agriculture that represents the land.

The third is that the earth was thought to be stable and the sun to revolve around it in earlier times before the technology was established. Later on, it was later discovered that it was the other way around. It was difficult to directly express this fact to those who believed in old knowledge. The light of Islam might not reach as many individuals if this path were taken. By using a literary expression, Prophet Muhammad (PBUH) satisfied the people of that time with his response.

When the earth revolves around the sun, it passes through twelve imaginary circles (twelve constellations). These are referred to as zodiacal signs. The ox and the fish are two of these signs. At various times, Prophet Muhammad (PBUH) was asked what the earth is situated on. He responded the first time: on the ox, and the second time: on the fish. He thus informed fourteen centuries before that the earth passes through the constellations of ox and fish, but that the sun does not revolve around the earth, but rather the earth revolves around the sun.

Prophet Mohammad (PBUH) expressed three great truths in a metaphorical and allusive manner, satisfying his addressees both in that century and in subsequent centuries.

The hadith, which is frequently brought up by various circles to defame Islam, is actually one of the miracles of our Prophet (PBUH).

Whatever he (PBUH) said is true. For those who can understand...

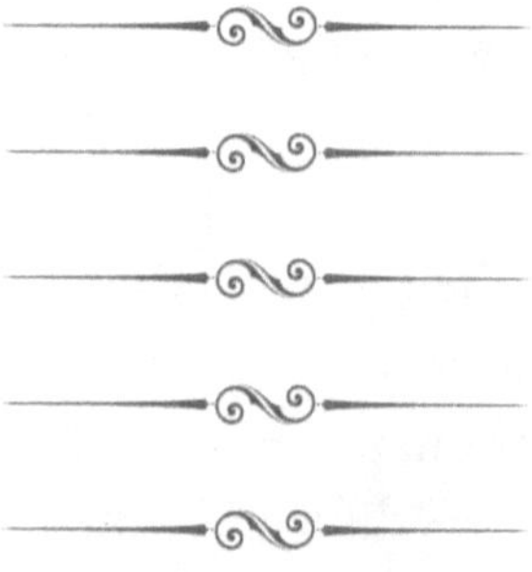

If No One Could See, Why Did God Create Galaxies?

God creates countless living things. Some live for one day. Maybe under the sea, under the ground, in the forests, in the deserts, there are creatures that people never know.

He creates planets, solar systems, galaxies. People can't see them, they can't step on them. They cannot travel there because they are far away. If they can do, they will die as soon as they get close.

Maybe there are beings on the stars that are like the animals on earth and can survive in the conditions of that place.

Why did Allah create a planet 70 billion light years away that we do not know, or a creature we have never seen under the ocean?

Answer: There are beings who see celestial bodies, even live there. These are angels and spiritual beings.

Assuming that there may exist stars that even angels have not seen;

Allah himself is the spectator of this universe. He watches the universe He created and the works of art.

From this, so to speak, Allah takes (in a form befitting the sacredness and perfect self-sufficiency of the necessarilyexistence essence) (in a form worthy of Him) a boundless holy pleasure and an infinite sacred delight.

No attribute of Allah resembles the attributes of creatures. Allah's seeing and hearing are not like our seeing or hearing, just as His delight and pleasure are not like ours or anything else.

All of Allah's attributes, which are used in common with His creatures, are of a nature that we do not know about far above creatures.

Almighty Allah, in all His attributes and names, is never like the world of the created. The fact that Allah characterizes Himself with names and attributes such as power, knowledge, will, life, sight and hearing in the Qur'an indicates these qualities exist in a unique way to Him. However, it does not explain how these qualities are in divine existence.

God does not need eyes for sight, ears for hearing, hands for power, tongue for speaking, and body for life.

I refer those who are curious about these issues to my book "Can God Create a Rock He cannot Lift?".

As for the matter of a being living and dying for a short time; If that entity lives in a moment, if it lives in 1 million years, it is considered having gained eternity. Because it is in Allah's pre-eternal knowledge.

Conclusion

I've tried to convey the scenes of the Apocalypse described in the Qur'an by using today's space science scientific discoveries. Since we have not witnessed a terrible event such as Doomsday, we can partly predict how it will happen, but we cannot feel it. Our efforts are limited only to scientific knowledge. How will time work at Doomsday, and how will people who perish live in that moment?

The old tribes, who went beyond the limit, were destroyed. The most extensive destruction of this ummah will be with Doomsday. Not just a town or country, but the whole world will be destroyed. Even the stars will fall and the heavens will collapse.

Doomsday is closer to us than the tip of our noses. The apocalypse is only a matter of time.

God created the universe opening like a rosebud. In the same way, all galaxies and skies will be closed like rose petals.

The scientific community believed in matter's pre-eternity. Later, it was discovered that the universe is expanding, just as the Qur'an expresses. Because the universe is expanding, going back in time reveals that the universe began from a single point. Calculations revealed that the "single point" containing all of the universe's matter must have zero volume and infinite density.

The universe was created as a result of the explosion of this zero-volume point. In fact, zero volume is a theoretical expression of this subject. Science can only use the expression 'point at zero volume' to describe the concept of 'absence,' which is beyond the human mind's comprehension limits. 'A point of zero volume' actually means 'absence.' The universe came into existence out of nothing (was created) just as the Quran states.

Allah, who created the universe from nothing, can certainly destroy it. And he can recreate it.

If the world of science were to simulate an apocalypse in which black holes could cause across our solar system and galaxy, what we would see and hear would confirm the statements of the Qur'an. Because the Qur'an is the word of Allah who sees all times (at the same time). As science progresses, it may find new and more terrifying doomsday machines. But the apocalyptic scenes described in the Qur'an do not change.

Allah, who created this huge universe and informs us in the Qur'an how He created it, has also revealed that He will destroy it. Advances in astronomy confirm the Quran as to how the universe came into being. So the destruction of the universe will undoubtedly happen as the Quran foretold.

Don't miss out!

Visit the website below and you can sign up to receive emails whenever ahmet yazici publishes a new book. There's no charge and no obligation.

https://books2read.com/r/B-A-XNWH-BYOAC

BOOKS2READ

Connecting independent readers to independent writers.

Did you love *Big Crunch: Invisible Apocalyptic Machines*? Then you should read *An Islamic Approach to Time Travel*[1] by ahmet yazici!

[2]

Is time travel possible? Can man travel to the future or the past? Or can one travel to new dimensions by discovering new devices?

The most general definition of time travel is the ability to travel to any time period or location of your choosing based on your own decisions. While science anticipates the issue, Sufism has been quietly living this experience within itself for 1000s of years, counting the saints in previous nations.

---

1. https://books2read.com/u/4Xwa1e

2. https://books2read.com/u/4Xwa1e

In this material world, we are living a life of limited knowledge and experience, enslaved to worldliness. A century ago, technologies such as mobile phones, television, and the internet were considered to be quite far-fetched and impossible technologies and science fiction stories. So is a phenomenon like time travel. Although this has not been proven in terms of science, films made, books written, and articles published on this subject for years show that it is not impossible to travel in time.

Leaving the part of the issue that concerns science to science, I will deal with the Islamic and Sufi and logical aspects.

This work, which I have supported with the lived saints' stories, is also the first work I published in the year 2023. I hope you will like it.

About the Author

Ahmet Yazici lives in Turkey with his parents and brother. He likes to write non-fiction Islamic works that prove the truths of faith in a rational way and fiction works (primarily fantasy fiction).